Teaching With the Rib-Tickling Poetry of Douglas Florian

BY DOUGLAS FLORIAN AND JOAN NOVELLI

NEW YORK · TORONTO · LONDON · AUCKLAND · SYDNEY
MEXICO CITY · NEW DELHI · HONG KONG · BUENOS AIRES

SCHOLASTIC
Teaching
Resources

Contents

About This Book

The poems in this book are packed with invitations to explore sound and letter relationships, vocabulary, grammar and mechanics, math and science concepts, and more! Here's a sampling of ways in which this collection can enrich and enliven teaching across your curriculum:

◆ phonics ("The Summer Trees," page 72, has flocks and flocks of birds—and consonant clusters.)

◆ spelling ("Back to School," page 8, will have students "thinking" about spelling patterns—like the ending -ing.)

◆ parts of speech ("A Monster's Day," page 23, is all about action verbs.)

◆ vocabulary (Use "Great Skates," page 35, to explore new vocabulary for overused words.)

◆ number and operations ("What," page 24, makes monstrous fun out of practicing addition and subtraction skills.)

◆ multiplication ("Valentine's Day," page 40, introduces a delicious way to explore patterns in multiplication.)

◆ science connections ("The Caterpillar," page 12, invites investigations of life cycles and nutrition.)

POETRY collaboration

Invite your students to illustrate a book of poetry by Douglas Florian! As you share the poems in this book with children, write them on chart paper and let children copy them into books they make, then illustrate them. For a fancier book, guide children in following these steps:
1. Stack the pages, then punch six holes along the left side.
2. "Stitch" a binding with ribbon, threading it through the holes.
3. Knot the ribbon at the top, then tie a bead to each end.
Encourage children to bring their books home throughout the year to share their growing poetry collections with their families.

All About

Douglas Florian

I was born and grew up in New York City. That means I'm a native New Yorker. When I was a kid, I used to watch my father paint and draw. Later I studied painting and drawing in an art school. After I graduated, I did many drawings for *The New York Times*. I then started illustrating children's books, first those written by other people, but later I wrote my own. Most of my recent books are poetry. For me a poem can be playful. I like to make up words like *snoozepaper* (a newspaper that puts you to sleep) or *flycycle* (a bicycle that flies). Sometimes I put words ǝpᴉsdn uʍop or sdrawkcab. I also like to give shape to some poems. I wrote a poem about an anteater which snakes across the page like an anteater's long tongue. Speaking of snakes, I created a poem about a python and the poem coils around itself.

Here are some questions children ask me:

Where do you get your ideas?

I get many ideas from nonfiction books, like field guides. One day I read that a starfish doesn't have a brain. I put that fact in my poem "The Starfish" (from *In the Swim*). I even get ideas from a dictionary. Did you know the word *caterpillar* comes from the ancient Latin words *catta*, which means "cat," and "pilus," which means "hair"? In ancient Rome, people thought a caterpillar was a hairy cat. How about that!

How can you rhyme all the time?

I go through the alphabet to make rhyming words. (What rhymes with *cat? Bat, fat, hat, mat,* and *gnat!*) For longer rhymes, I use a rhyming dictionary. Then you can rhyme *cat* with *acrobat* and *diplomat!* You can even spell words wrong. That's called poetic license and I renew mine every year! So, in my poem about a lynx I say it "stynx" that some people use a lynx for fur.

What are your favorite animals to draw?

I have two: the frog and the elephant. I guess my favorite is the frogelephant! I love to use different media. I create with pencil, pen and ink, watercolor, gouache (an opaque watercolor), and tempera paint. Sometimes I use watercolor paper. I've even used brown paper bags! (Those pictures are in *insectlopedia*.)

There's only one other thing I want you to know about writing poems: HAVE FUN!

Doug Florian

Tip

What rhymes with *wait*? *Eight*, *Kate*, and *precipitate*! To assist students in creating rhyming lines, share **The Scholastic Rhyming Dictionary**, by Sue Young (Scholastic, 1997). This child-friendly reference is organized by vowel sounds and final syllables and features more than 15,000 words. Or check an online rhyming reference, such as **www. rhymezone.com**.

Teaching Activities for Any Time

Words to Know

Some of the poems in this book will introduce children to new vocabulary. Whether it's silly (*fatterpillar*; page 12) or not (*optometrists*; page 16), take time to let children tell what they know about the word and learn more about it. As appropriate, invite children to share words with a similar meaning. For example, they might suggest *likes* or *prefers* for *favors* (from "Flower Power," page 64).

Morning Meeting Poetry Break

Make poetry part of your morning meeting routine. You might set aside time one day a week to make it a special occasion. Invite a child to choose the morning meeting poem from those you've already introduced. (Copy the poems on a flip chart and keep them near the morning meeting area so children can easily flip through them as they make their choices.) Let the child tell what he or she likes best about the chosen poem, and then lead the class in a choral reading.

Make It New

Write a poem on chart paper. Use sticky notes to cover up one word in a pair of rhyming words. Invite children to suggest replacement words. Copy the new words on sticky notes (one per sticky note). Put them in place and read the new poem!

Make-Your-Own Bookmarks

Page 7 features a reproducible bookmark that will put poetry at your students' fingertips whenever they pick up a book. Give each child a copy of the bookmark page and read "Book Look" together. To make the bookmark, cut out the pattern and spread glue on the back. Fold on the dashed line, being careful to match up the edges. Let children write one of their favorite poems on the blank side.

Shapes, Sounds, Rhythms, and Rhymes

Let children use the poems in this book as models for writing their own. Share these tips for more inspiration:

◆ Let the information you gather help you write the poem—for example, a poem about inchworms arches across the page like the insect. (See "The Inchworm," page 61.) Does a certain shape work with your poem?

◆ Listen to the sound of the words you choose. Do they create a rhythm that feels right?

◆ Tap out the rhythm of your words on your desk. Don't be afraid to move words around to change the rhythm.

Poetry Bookmark

Book Look

Open a book and
Turn the pages.
It's a fun thing
For all ages.
Read a story
Find a poem.
A book is where
Your mind can roam.

—Douglas Florian

Back to School

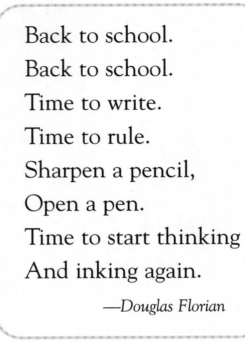

Back to school.
Back to school.
Time to write.
Time to rule.
Sharpen a pencil,
Open a pen.
Time to start thinking
And inking again.

—Douglas Florian

Word Hunt

Can students spot a word in this poem that names part of their body? *(back)* After they find it, ask them to tell what the word means in this poem. *(to, toward,* or *in a place from which a person or thing came)* Can they think of any other meanings for this word? *(a playing position in sports)* Now let students hunt for other words in the poem that have the same sound as words they know. Notice that some of these words have the same sound *and* spelling. For example, the word *rule* refers to measurement; it can also refer to a king's job. The word *pen* is a writing instrument in the poem; it can also be a pig's home. Other words have the same sound but different meaning and spelling. For example, the word *to* in the poem sounds like *too* and *two* but has a different meaning. The word *write* sounds like *right* but has a different meaning and spelling.

TEACHING Connections

- back to school
- homonyms, homographs
- inflectional endings

The Ultimate Eraser Test

Pencils with fresh erasers are a sure sign of the start of the school year. But are all erasers equal? Find out with this fun test:

◆ Start by sharing a poem about pencils:

Pencilly

The pencil is a splendid thing
For which there's no replacer.
But better than the pencil is
The little pink eraser.

—*Douglas Florian*

◆ Create an eraser display (including a little pink eraser) and let students browse it, looking and touching, but not testing. Which eraser do they think will erase best? Worst?

◆ Set up a station for testing each eraser. Include the eraser, a pencil, and paper.

◆ Have children rotate through the stations in small groups, testing and rating each eraser, and recording comments on a sheet of paper.

◆ Bring students together to share results. Do they agree on which one works best? If necessary, choose the top three or four performers and run another test to find the ultimate eraser.

LANGUAGE ARTS

Thinking and Inking

"Time to start thinking and inking again..." What other -ing words go with the start of a new school year? Use the poem to introduce spelling patterns for inflectional endings.

◆ Give each child a copy of the poem framework on page 11. Let students complete the poem by adding five words that end in -ing and say something about "back to school." Encourage creativity. Words like *friend-making*, *bus-taking*, and *lunch-line-waiting* can work just as well as *listening*, *reading*, and *test-taking*.

◆ Let children share their new poems. List their new -ing words on the chalkboard.

◆ Together, look for spelling patterns. For example, students may discover that they double the final consonant in one-syllable words with a short vowel, such as *sit (sitting)*, and drop the final -e before adding -ing in words such as *smile (smiling)*.

Tip

For more teaching activities that are just right for the start of the school year, see *Fresh & Fun: Back to School* by Joan Novelli (Scholastic Professional Books, 2001). This book of interdisciplinary activities includes games, hands-on math and science activities, pocket-chart ideas, reproducible pages, literature connections, and a big, colorful poetry poster to extend your back-to-school poetry fun.

BOOK break

Students heading back to school may be toting the usual supplies, such as pencils and paper, but how about a mouse? In *If You Take a Mouse to School*, by Laura Joffe Numeroff (HarperCollins, 2002), the best-loved mouse from *If You Give a Mouse a Cookie* and *If You Take a Mouse to the Movies* is back and behaving in familiar ways. First it's a lunchbox he wants, along with a sandwich and a snack. Then he needs a notebook and some pencils, and a backpack to stash it all in. The mouse dives right in at school. Can your students spell *precocious* and *adrenaline*? How about *insidious*? This mouse can (of course).

Back to School

Name _____   Date _____

Back to School

Back to school.
Time to write.
Time to rule.
Sharpen a pencil,
Open a pen.
Time to start thinking
And inking and

_____ and

_____ and

_____ and

_____ and

_____ and

_____ and

_____ again.

Extra! Can you make two words in your poem rhyme?

The Caterpillar

She eats eight leaves at least
To fill her,
Which leaves her like a
Fatterpillar,
Then rents a room inside
A pupa,
And checks out: Madame Butterfly—
How super!

—*Douglas Florian*

TEACHING Connections

◆ homophones
◆ life cycles
◆ nutrition

Write the word *ate* on the chalkboard. Can students find a word in the poem that sounds the same? Invite a volunteer to use a pointer to identify the word. (line 1: *eight*) Have students notice how the words sound the same but have different spellings. Can they find another word like this in the poem? (*to*) Brainstorm other words that sound the same but have different spellings. (For more fun with homophones, share *Good Night, Good Knight*. See Book Break, page 13.)

LANGUAGE ARTS ◆ SCIENCE

Life Cycle Stories

Make double-sided books to compare a child's life cycle with that of a butterfly.

◆ Investigate the life cycle of a butterfly. (*egg, pupa, chrysalis, butterfly*) Let children name the stages of their own life cycle. (*baby, child, adult, senior citizen*)

◆ Give each child four copies of page 15. Have children cut apart the pages and stack them in two sets of four.

◆ Have children complete and illustrate one set of pages to show the life cycle of a butterfly. Have them do the same with the second set of pages to show a child's life cycle.

◆ Give each child a sheet of construction paper. Have children place the butterfly life cycle pages in order on the left, and their own life cycle pages in order on the right. Have children top each stack of pages with a construction-paper cover, and staple as shown to bind.

BOOK break

Good Night, Good Knight, by Shelley Moore Thomas (Dutton, 2000), is a high-spirited story of a knight on watch who gallops through the forest to investigate large, loud roars. Each time, he finds three little dragons all ready for bed—except that they need a drink of water, then a story, a song, another drink, and, eventually, a good-night kiss on their scaly little cheeks. Repetitive text, rhyming words ("crumbly tumbly tower"), and a surprise ending make this a favorite read-aloud. And, of course, the wordplay (good *night*, good *knight*) invites classroom explorations of homophones.

SCIENCE ◆ LANGUAGE ARTS

Leaves for Lunch

The caterpillar in the poem ate eight leaves—at least! That kind of nutrition may be just right for a caterpillar, but what about for a child?

Share *Butterfly Story* (below) to learn more about the nutritional needs of a caterpillar. Then compare children's nutritional needs. Ask: "What foods do you need to eat in order to grow?" Set up a four-column chart to sort the foods they name: "Sweets and Fats," "Meat, Fish, Poultry, Eggs, Dried Beans, Nuts," "Milk, Yogurt, Cheese," and "Bread, Cereal, Grains, Pasta." Use the food pyramid to learn more about nutritional needs. (You can download a copy at **www.usda.gov**.)

BOOK break

Butterfly Story, by Anca Hariton (Dutton, 1995), follows the life cycle of a butterfly from a tiny green egg sticking to a nettle leaf to a colorful butterfly soaring above the trees. Soft watercolor illustrations in delicate colors detail the science behind one of nature's most wondrous events.

LANGUAGE ARTS

Cat, Pat, Rat

The caterpillar may not be a cat, but there is a *cat* in *caterpillar*. Can students find it?

Write the word *caterpillar* on the chalkboard, and invite a volunteer to underline the word *cat*. Now challenge children to find other little words in the big word—including *at*, *ate*, *I*, *pill*, *pillar*, *ill*, and *a*.

Watch
Me Grow!

I'm a/an _____

What things can I do?

I can _____, _____, and _____.

To name just a few!

Name _____

Watch
Me Grow!

I'm a/an _____

What things can I do?

I can _____, _____, and _____.

To name just a few!

Name _____

Today's Weather

Rain, hail,
Garbage pails.
Snow, sleet,
Chicken feet.
Drizzle, mist,
Optometrists.
Cloudy, showers,
Cauliflowers.
Later clearing
With an earring.

—*Douglas Florian*

TEACHING Connections

◆ vocabulary
◆ weather
◆ communication skills

Word Hunt

Rain, hail, snow, sleet…. Invite students to find words for weather conditions in this poem. What other words for weather do students know? Record their words on chart paper and display for reference. Then have students work in pairs to write new lines for the poem. Students can select any two weather words they like, then pair them with a silly rhyming line like the ones in the poem. For example, they might pair *downpour* and *drops* with *ice cream pops*, or *cats* and *dogs* with *polliwogs*.

SCIENCE ◆ LANGUAGE ARTS

And Now for the Weather

After reading aloud the poem with children, try this:

Invite children to take turns reading the poem aloud as though they were delivering the weather report on the news. (They may have a little trouble keeping a straight face.) For a more serious look at the weather, let students take turns sharing the day's weather during the morning meeting. In the case of precipitation, have them use words from the poem and chart to most precisely describe the weather.

MOVEMENT

Making Rain

Add sound effects to a reading of the poem.

Have children practice the following sound effects in groups, choosing an "arrangement" that best fits the language and mood of the poem: slide hands back and forth, slap knees, tap fingers on table, tap feet, clap hands, and stomp feet. Read the poem aloud several times to let each group perform the sound effects.

LANGUAGE ARTS ◆ ART ◆ SCIENCE

What We Know

This weather poem introduces rain, snow, and clouds. Let children show what they know about each with this collaborative project.

Have children trace and cut out raindrop, snowflake, and cloud shapes. Ask them to write something they know about each weather condition on the corresponding shape. Display a sheet of white mural paper. Let children combine their shapes to make three scenes: a rainstorm, a snowstorm, and a cloudy day. Have them add other elements to complete each scene.

BOOK break

For more fun with precipitation, share **Little Cloud**, by Eric Carle (Philomel, 1996). Little Cloud is a sheep, an airplane, and two trees, then gets together with other clouds to make rain.

Tip

Pencils and foil pie pans are also good "rainmakers." Children can tap the back of the pan with a pencil to make sound effects for a drizzle, sprinkle, or downpour.

Made in the Shade

The shade in the shadow of an old oak tree
Is wide as an elephant's hide and me.

—*Douglas Florian*

Word Hunt

This two-line poem and its title are full of long- and short-vowel sounds. Play a matching game to make sound-spelling connections. Start by saying the word *shade*. Ask: "Can you find another word in the poem that has the same *a* sound?" (*made*) Repeat with the words *in* (short *i*), *shadow* (short *a*), *old* (long *o*), and *wide* (long *i*). Write each word on the chalkboard, grouping like-vowel sounds together. Let students suggest other words that have the same vowel sounds and add them to the lists. Focus attention on *made, shade, wide,* and *hide* to reinforce the silent *e* spelling pattern. Let children suggest other spelling patterns they notice in any of the word groups.

TEACHING connections

- vowel sounds
- simile
- measurement

LANGUAGE ARTS

Wide as an Elephant's Hide

How wide is the shade of the old oak tree? Discuss how making comparisons like this helps readers create pictures in their minds.

Ask students to compare "the shade of an old oak tree" to something in the classroom that might be about as wide—for example, "as wide as the distance from the door to the bookshelf." Reread the poem to see how the poet described the shade ("as wide as an elephant's hide and me"). Explain that these kinds of comparisons are called similes. Invite students to go on a simile hunt to find examples in books they've read. Let them write the similes they find on sentence strips (along with the book title and author) and add them to a bulletin board display.

BOOK break

To see how other authors use similes to create sensory-rich images, share *Owl Moon*, by Jane Yolen (Philomel, 1987). Poetic language, such as "and when their voices faded away it was as quiet as a dream," sets just the right mood for a peaceful nighttime walk in the woods.

MATH ◆ SCIENCE ◆ LANGUAGE ARTS

Shady Measurements

How wide is the shade of a tree (or some other object) outside the school?

Give pairs of children a length of string. Gather children around a tree and let them take turns using the string to measure the tree's shade (or shadow) from one end to the other. Have children cut their string accordingly. Back in the classroom, challenge children to find something that is the same size as their string—for example, it may be as wide as three of their tables, or as four children standing side by side, arms outstretched. Have children complete and illustrate the following simile to compare the shade of the tree to their non-standard measurement:

The shade in the shadow of _____

Is as wide as _____.

Monster Home

A monster made its very home
Inside the middle of this poem.
This monster loved to gobble words—

Of this poor poem it ate two-thirds.

—*Douglas Florian*

Tell students you're thinking of three words in the poem that have something in common. Can children guess which words they are? Let students guess until they come up with *middle*, *gobble*, and *poor*: These words all have double letters. Words with double letters are fun for children to spell. (Children get to say "m, i, double d, l, e" instead of "m, i, d, d, l, e"— which is a much more special way to spell the word!) How many more double letter words do students know? Start with students' own names. (Is there a *Harry*, *Billy*, or *Anna* in the class?) Now have students look around the room and name double letter words they see. Noticing features of words such as double letters can help children remember how to spell them. Have them try the same with their weekly spelling words.

TEACHING connections

- ◆ spelling patterns
- ◆ fractions
- ◆ synonyms

MATH ◆ ART

Monster Meals

How big would the poem have been if the monster hadn't eaten two-thirds of it? Let children share their answers and, especially, their reasoning. For example, a child might count the lines (4) and reason that the poem might have been 6 lines long. (4 equals two-thirds of 6) Then let students pretend to be hungry monsters with this activity:

◆ Give children coupon inserts and grocery store circulars. Have them cut out pictures of foods they'd like to eat—for example, pizza, cookies, apples, and bread.

◆ Let each child select a food picture. Give everyone a handful of play clay. (See recipe, right.) Have children make their food with the clay.

◆ Call out a fraction of the food that the "monster" will eat—for example, two-thirds—and have children divide the food accordingly.

◆ Let children walk around the room to see how their classmates divided each food. Repeat the activity, letting children select a new food to make and giving them a new fraction to work with.

LANGUAGE ARTS

Language for Lunch

Gobble...It doesn't just mean eat.
It means gulp, cram, and stuff!

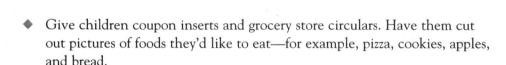

Invite students to think of all the ways they could eat their lunch. They could gobble it, or they might nibble, attack, inhale, pick at, put away, or savor their lunch. Build vocabulary with the mini-thesaurus on page 22. Give each child a copy. Have children cut apart the pages, then stack them in order and staple. Invite children to complete the rhyme on the cover. Then have them complete pages 2–4 with descriptive words for the ways they might eat. Have children illustrate each page. Then let them share their books with partners. Finally, bring the class together to see how many different words for *eat* there are! Chart them for a class reference.

Tip

Play Clay

Here's an easy recipe for perfect play clay. Store it in resealable bags when not in use.

◆ Mix 6 drops food coloring with 3 cups water.

◆ Mix water, 3 cups flour, 3 tablespoons vegetable oil, 3 tablespoons cream of tartar, and $1\frac{1}{2}$ cups salt in a pan.

◆ Cook over medium heat, stirring constantly, until a dough forms (about five minutes).

◆ Let cool, and knead until smooth.

Language for Lunch

You can _____ your food.

You can _____ it, too.

These words both mean eat.

How else can you chew?

Name _____

1

Synonym for Eat: _____

Definition: _____

_____

_____

2

Synonym for Eat: _____

Definition: _____

_____

_____

3

Synonym for Eat: _____

Definition: _____

_____

_____

4

A Monster's Day

Monsters creep and monsters crawl
Monsters bite and monsters brawl
Monsters steal and monsters snatch
Monsters hurt and monsters hatch
Monsters smack and monsters smash
Monsters tease and monsters trash
Monsters grab and monsters groan
Monsters mash and monsters moan
A monster's day is never through
With all those monstrous things to do.

—*Douglas Florian*

Creep, *crawl, brawl*…. How many action verbs can children find in "A Monster's Day"? Write the poem on chart paper and send children searching. Say the words together, enjoying the alliterative language of each pair of action verbs: *creep* and *crawl*, *bite* and *brawl*, *steal* and *snatch*, *hurt* and *hatch*, *smack* and *smash*, *tease* and *trash*, *grab* and *groan*, *mash* and *moan*. Let children pair up to dramatically interpret the words in a class read-aloud. Read the last two lines together for a strong finish! Give children copies of page 25. Invite them to fill in the blanks with more action verbs to create a new version of the poem.

TEACHING connections

- ◆ action verbs
- ◆ synonyms
- ◆ alliteration

LANGUAGE ARTS

A Monstrous Word Wall

Children are barely back at school before they're talking about Halloween. Use their enthusiasm to teach thesaurus skills and build a "monstrous" vocabulary.

After reading aloud the poem, ask children which word means the same thing as *huge.* (*monstrous*) Let children practice using the word *monstrous* in their own sentences. Then brainstorm other words with a similar meaning—for example, *immense, enormous, gigantic,* and *colossal.* Divide the class into teams and have each choose one of the words. Ask each team to create a poster that illustrates the word. Display students' monstrous words to make a handy and visually appealing reference for writing.

MATH ◆ ART

Monster Math

Introduce a new poem about a monstrous creature. Then practice addition and subtraction skills with monstrous numbers.

◆ Share "What" (left) by Douglas Florian.

◆ Give each child a copy of page 26. Have children complete the blanks without solving the equations—for example, "7 + 4 = _____ mouths." (You may want to specify a range of numbers from which students may choose.) There are two blank body parts for children to fill in as they like.

◆ Have children trade papers and solve each other's problems, and then create monsters with as many body parts as each answer indicates.

What

What has fourteen hairy legs?
What lays purple pointed eggs?
What has spines along its back?
What eats children for a snack?
What is more than ten feet tall?
What has eyes like basketballs?
What has seven swirling tails?
What has poison on its nails?
What has stringy, long green hairs?
I don't know, but it's coming upstairs!

—Douglas Florian

BOOK break

For more monstrous fun, share **The Iron Giant: A Story in Five Nights**, by Ted Hughes (Knopf, 1999). Your students will enjoy this great read-aloud in the days leading up to Halloween. **I Spy Spooky Night**, by Jean Marzollo (Scholastic, 1999) is always a favorite, too, with rhyming text that invites readers to find hidden objects on each page.

A Monster's Day

Name _____   Date _____

Use "A Monster's Day" to make a new poem. Fill in the blanks
on each line with words that start with the same sound—for
example, *growl* and *grin*. Try to use a different sound on each line.

A Monster's Day

Monsters _____ and monsters _____

Monsters _____ and monsters _____

Monsters _____ and monsters _____

Monsters _____ and monsters _____

Monsters _____ and monsters _____

Monsters _____ and monsters _____

Monsters _____ and monsters _____

Monsters _____ and monsters _____

A monster's day is never through

With all those monstrous things to do.

—*retold by* _____

Teaching With the Rib-Tickling Poetry of Douglas Florian   Scholastic Teaching Resources

Monster Math

Name _____   Date _____

Fill in the blanks for each equation but do not solve the problem. Trade papers with a classmate and complete the number sentences. Draw the monster using the answers!

_____ + _____ = _____ heads

_____ + _____ = _____ eyes

_____ − _____ = _____ mouths

_____ + _____ = _____ legs

_____ − _____ = _____ arms

_____ + _____ = _____ hands

_____ − _____ = _____ fingers

_____ − _____ = _____ tails

_____ − _____ = _____ _____

_____ + _____ = _____ _____

Teaching With the Rib-Tickling Poetry of Douglas Florian   Scholastic Teaching Resources

Windblown

One cold November day
The wind blew my wool hat away.
I glued it back onto my head,
But then my head flew off instead.

—*Douglas Florian*

Tip

Check the weather anywhere at **www.accuweather.com**.

The wind blew away the hat in this poem. Can students find a word in the poem that has something in common with the word *blew*? How about *flew*? Identify these words as "action words," or verbs. Look at the way these words change, depending on the tense: *blow, blew, blown; fly, flew, flown.* Guide students to recognize that the way these verbs change is different from the way many verbs change. Brainstorm other words with a similar pattern of irregular changes, such as *grow/grew/grown, throw/threw/thrown,* and *know/knew/known.*

Word Hunt

TEACHING Connections
- irregular verbs/spelling
- seasons
- weather

SOCIAL STUDIES ◆ SCIENCE

Where in the World?

After sharing the poem with students, investigate where in the world it might be a cold, windy day.

The answer might be right where you live, or it may be somewhere on the other side of the country. Invite students to work with partners to investigate the weather that day, using a newspaper or an Internet resource. Have students share their answers, telling what the weather conditions are in their cold, windy part of the world and locating the area on a map.

MATH ◆ SCIENCE

Best Guess

Which day in November will be the coldest? Have fun guessing with this estimation activity:

◆ Before the first of the month, invite children to sign their names to a calendar to indicate their best guess. Have them record an estimated temperature, too.

◆ Discuss patterns in students' guesses: At what time of the month do most students think it will be coldest? (*beginning*, *middle*, *end*) Why? Do more students think it will be coldest during the first half or the second half?

◆ Let a child check the temperature at the same time each day. Provide this information for weekends. Discuss results at the end of the month.

MATH

Calendar Hats

This appealing, interactive class calendar helps students brush up on addition and subtraction skills:

◆ Cut out 30 hats. (You can enlarge and use the patterns on page 29.) Write the numbers for each day of the month on a hat (one number per hat).

◆ Give each child a hat. Have children write a number sentence on the blank side of the hat that matches the number on the other side. Display the hats on a bulletin board, equation side facing out, along with the name of the month.

◆ Each day, ask students to find the hat with a number sentence that equals the date. Have a volunteer turn over the hat to check the answer. (On Mondays, do this for three hats to include the weekend dates.)

Tip

For a challenge, invite students to use the data they gathered to make predictions about the next month. Encourage students to incorporate what they know about that month/season to make the best guess.

Calendar Hats

What I Love About Winter

Frozen lakes
Hot pancakes
Lots of snow
Hot cocoa
Skates and skis
Evergreen trees
Funny hats
Thermostats
Sunset blaze
Holidays
Snowball fights
Fireplace nights
Chimneys steaming
Winter dreaming

—*Douglas Florian*

TEACHING connections

- ◆ **compound words**
- ◆ **creative thinking**
- ◆ **measurement (temperature)**

Word Hunt

Pancakes, evergreen, sunset, snowball, fireplace . . . . This poem is packed with compound words. Introduce compound words by writing the word *pancakes* on the chalkboard. Let children find the two words that make up this word. When children have found the words *pan* and *cake*, ask them to tell how the two words relate to the meaning of the big word. (*A pancake is a kind of cake that's made in a pan.*) Let children repeat this activity with the other compound words in the poem. Help students recognize that this strategy can sometimes help them pronounce and understand new words.

LANGUAGE ARTS

Making a List

"What I Love About Winter" is a list poem—the poet lists things he loves about winter. Invite students to make a list of things they love about winter. Have them give their lists a name and illustrate them. Display students' list poems on a bulletin board or bind them to make a book. Then play this game to have more fun with lists:

◆ The poet listed things he loves about winter. What other kinds of lists do people make? There are grocery lists, "to do" lists, birthday lists, guest lists, and more. Write list categories on slips of paper. Place them in a paper bag.

◆ Invite a volunteer to select a category from the bag at random. Read aloud the category, then challenge children to make a list that fits the description. For example, if the category is "Things in the Classroom That Start With the Letter *B*," students might list books, backpacks, bookshelves, binders, buttons, blocks, bean plants, and so on.

◆ Let children share the items on their lists and figure out how many different items in all are on their lists. Invite children to choose a favorite list topic to create a poem!

MATH

Hot and Cold

Some of the items listed in the poem are hot. Some are not! Ask students what they think is the hottest item on the list. The coldest? Then ask them to guess the hottest place in the school. The coldest? Divide the class into groups to check.

Assign each group a location in the school. Give each group a thermometer. Review how to read a thermometer. Have students place their thermometers at the designated locations. Allow time for the thermometer to register the correct temperature in each location. Have children check the thermometers (at the same time) and record the temperature of each location. Repeat the procedure several times during the week. Let children average the temperatures for each location and share their results with the class. What is the hottest spot in the school? The coldest? What could account for the differences?

Tip

Have children make more math connections by graphing or charting the data they gather. Use each graphic organizer to make more comparisons.

Moon Boon

When the moon is just a sickle,
Then it eats a sour pickle.
When the moon shines like a crescent,
How it feasts upon a pheasant.
As it grows in size to half,
It consumes a whole giraffe.
While the moon becomes three-quarters,
Fifteen tons of fish it orders.
Later in its gibbous phase
Swallows whales with mayonnaise,
Till at last it's full and great,
Cleared the sky and cleaned its plate.
Everything in sight it ate.
Now it's time for losing weight.

—*Douglas Florian*

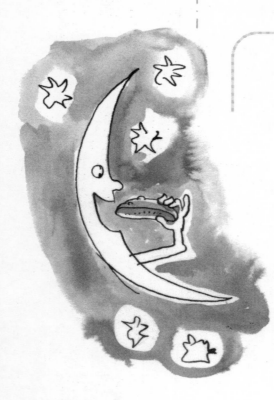

TEACHING connections

- moon phases
- calendars
- shapes

Word Hunt

Is the word *sickle* new for any of your students? Guide students in looking up this word in a dictionary that includes a picture. Have children notice the shape. Does the moon ever look like this? Together, find other words in the poem that refer to phases of the moon: *crescent, half, three-quarters, gibbous,* and *full.* To learn more about the phases of the moon, and see how they correspond to the language in the poem, see Moon Match (page 33).

SCIENCE

Moon Match

For a fun look at moon phases, ask students: "What do you think the moon looks like when it orders fifteen tons of fish?"

Continue to explore the poetic descriptions of the moon's phases with page 34. Have children cut out the picture boxes at the bottom of the page. Reread the poem and have children match the pictures to the descriptions and glue them in place. Students will notice one empty picture box. Have them draw a picture of the moon when it is "just a sickle."

Cresent   Third Quarter   Gibbous   Full

LANGUAGE ARTS ◆ ART ◆ SCIENCE

"Moon Boon" Big Book

Invite children to creatively explore the moon's phases by making an illustrated Big Book version of the poem "Moon Boon."

Write the poem on chart paper and divide the class into seven groups. Have each group choose a set of lines to illustrate (1–2, 3–4, 5–6, 7–8, 9–10, 11–14). Have the remaining group handle the cover. Give each group a large sheet of drawing paper and let students decide how to work together to create their page. For example, one child might hand-letter the text (on a separate sheet of drawing paper, then paste it in place on the page), another might illustrate the moon in the sky, and a third might illustrate the "meal" (for example,"whales with mayonnaise"). Put students' completed pages together in order (laminate first for durability), and bind with O-rings or paper fasteners.

Tip

For pictures of the phases of the moon for each day of the month, go to **www.googol.com/ moon/**.

Moon Boon

Name _____   Date _____

When the moon is just a sickle,
Then it eats a sour pickle.

When the moon shines like a crescent,
How it feasts upon a pheasant.

As it grows in size to half,
It consumes a whole giraffe.

While the moon becomes three-quarters,
Fifteen tons of fish it orders.

Later in its gibbous phase
Swallows whales with mayonnaise,

Till at last it's full and great,
Cleared the sky and cleaned its plate.

Everything in sight it ate.
Now it's time for losing weight.

Crescent

Full

Third Quarter

Gibbous

Teaching With the Rib-Tickling Poetry of Douglas Florian   Scholastic Teaching Resources

Great Skates

> To skate is great.
> It's great to skate:
> A great big O
> Or figure 8.
> On ice it's nice
> To be precise.
> If I don't fall,
> It's nice times twice.
>
> —*Douglas Florian*

What word in the poem means double or two times something? (*twice*) After students identify the word, play a quick game of doubles: Take turns naming things that come in twos—for example, shoes, eyes, ears, wheels on a bicycle, covers on a book (front and back), and wings on a bird. Then try Nice Times Twice (page 37) for an activity that lets children combine times tables practice with artistic expression.

TEACHING Connections

- multiplication (twos)
- synonyms (for *nice*)
- spelling patterns

LANGUAGE ARTS

Not Nice!

Why did the poet use the word *nice* in the poem? (*It rhymes with precise and twice.*) If the poet didn't use a word that rhymed, what other words could he have used to express the same meaning?

Divide the class into pairs or groups of three to brainstorm synonyms for *nice*. After a set amount of time, let groups share their words. Copy the words on chart paper to make a class list. Display the list to inspire students to consider alternates for this word in their writing.

LANGUAGE ARTS ◆ MATH

Skating on Shaving Cream

Children may not be able to put on skates to experience making a "great big O or figure 8," but they can have fun "skating" in shaving cream.

◆ Squirt shaving cream on children's desks. Let them lather it up, and then "skate" with their fingers as you read aloud the poem, making great big Os and figure 8s.

◆ Choose a word from the poem that represents a word family—for example, *big.* Let children spell the word in the shaving cream, and then try other words with the same spelling pattern—for example, *dig, fig, jig, pig, rig, twig, wig.* Repeat with a new word family.

◆ Let children make up word problems based on the poem—for example, if three children in the class made great big Os on the ice, eight made figure 8s, and the rest just skated, how many just skated? Let students show their solution in the shaving cream.

MATH

Nice Times Twice

Learning doubles is a great strategy for memorizing multiplication facts. Use the poem to introduce doubles.

Ask children what in the poem is twice as nice. (*not falling when you skate*) Review the 2s times table to introduce doubling. Write each double as follows: twice two is …, twice three is …, twice four is …, and so on. Let each child choose a double to illustrate. Have children draw pictures of skaters in groups to represent each double.

$$2 \times 3 = 6$$

LANGUAGE ARTS ◆ HEALTH

Good Sport

Pair "Great Skates" with another poem by Douglas Florian about physical activity: "Good Sport" (right).

After sharing the poem, challenge students to find three words in the poem that were formed by following this rule: When a word ends with a silent *-e*, drop the *-e* before adding a suffix that starts with a vowel—for example, *skating, hiking,* and *biking*. Brainstorm other action words that follow this rule—for example, *dance, ride,* and *slide*. What are some that don't? (*walk, swim, skateboard, play*) Let pairs of children each choose a word from this group and develop a rule for adding the ending *-ing*. Have each group share their rule with the class.

BOOK break

What's one of the best ways to keep the flu from getting in the way of fun? Hand-washing! Share **Wash Your Hands!**, by Tony Ross (Kane/Miller, 2000), to reinforce this healthy habit. A princess resists washing her hands, but finally listens to the maid who explains that hand-washing will help keep the "germs and nasties" away. (And then, with clean hands, there's some nice cake to eat.) Follow up by having children trace their hands on paper, cut out the shapes, and write a hand-washing tip on them. Display the hands around the sink area to remind children of healthy hand-washing habits.

Good Sport

I love to ski.
I love to skate.
Inside a rink
My skating's great.

I'm good for golf.
I dig to dive.
On tennis courts
Of course I thrive.

I like long hiking,
Biking too.
Too bad I'm home
In bed with flu.

—*Douglas Florian*

Deep Freeze

On the coldest day of the year
I froze my nose and toes and ear.
And shin and chin and calf and thigh.
I didn't thaw until mid-July.

—*Douglas Florian*

Tip

Add movement to "Deep Freeze" to really involve children in the words. As you recite the poem together, touch the corresponding body parts: nose, toes, ear, shin, chin, calf, thigh. Try repeating the poem, a little faster each time. How fast can children recite the poem and keep up with the movements?

TEACHING connections

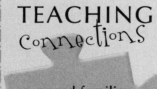

- word families
- median
- alliteration

Word Hunt

How many words with a long *i* sound can students find in the poem? Read the poem aloud, asking students to raise their hands each time they hear this sound. (*line 2 in the word* I, *line 3 in the word* thigh, *and line 4 in the words* I *and* July) Write the word *thigh* on the chalkboard and invite children to notice the letters that make the long -*i* sound (-*igh*). Brainstorm other words in this word family (*high, nigh, sigh*). Repeat the procedure with *July* (and the phonogram -*y*). Extend the activity by asking children to hunt for more long *i* words in books they're reading.

MATH ◆ LANGUAGE ARTS

In the Middle

When is "mid-July"? Challenge children to find out!

Have children tell what they think the word *mid* means. Then work together to come up with a definition. (*to be in the center or middle*) Provide calendars and let children work in pairs to determine the date that they think is mid-July. Let them share with the class their methods for determining the date. Discuss any different outcomes and work together to come up with an answer the class agrees on. Repeat the activity with other months and look for patterns. For a vocabulary-building connection, challenge children to find a word that means mid-month. (Hint: look up the word *ides*.)

LANGUAGE ARTS ◆ SCIENCE ◆ MOVEMENT

Melt Down

For a comparison, pair "Deep Freeze" with Douglas Florian's "Melt Down" (right). This poem makes lovely use of alliteration—in the words *sun, snowmen, sink, sound,* and (again) *snowmen.*

Copy the poem on chart paper and highlight the word *sun*. Invite children to take turns highlighting other words in the poem that start with the same sound. Ask children to describe the kind of feeling this repeated sound creates as they read the poem. (*The sound of the letter s is a soft sound— repeating it adds to the feeling of the snowmen melting silently.*) Go further by making a large sliding snowman-shaped tagboard thermometer. (A giant paper clip makes a good temperature indicator.) Review the temperature for freezing. Ask students at what temperature a snowman might begin melting. Have students pretend they are snowmen. As you move the temperature up and down, let them freeze or melt according to the change.

Melt Down

Beneath the sun
The snowmen melt.
They sink without a sound.
But snowmen never really die;
They just move underground.

—*Douglas Florian*

BOOK break

In **Henry and Mudge and the Snowman Plan**, by Cynthia Rylant (Simon & Schuster, 1999), there's a snowman-building contest, and Henry faces some tough competition. His father inspires an idea, and together they create a snowman that's worthy of the Most Original award.

Valentine's Day

Katie loves Billy,
But Billy loves Nan.
Nannie loves Eddie,
But Eddie loves Fran.
Frannie loves David,
But David loves Pat.
Pattie loves ice cream,
And so that is that.

—*Douglas Florian*

Copy the poem on chart paper. Read it aloud, and let children take turns highlighting all of the names. Ask: "What do all of these words have in common?" (*They are all names and they all start with a capital letter.*) Ask children to share what they know about capital letters. List the kinds of words that start with capital letters, including words that name specific people, places, and things. Invite children to suggest examples for each—for example, their names or initials, Earth, and the Statue of Liberty. Look around the room to name more. Students will find the months and days of the week capitalized on the calendar, geographic names capitalized on a map or globe, titles capitalized on books, and names of products capitalized on containers. For a follow-up activity, try the scavenger hunt on page 41.

TEACHING Connections

- proper nouns
- surveys
- multiplication

LANGUAGE ARTS

Capital Letters Scavenger Hunt

"Valentine's Day" has 17 words with capital letters. Thirteen of those words are names. Four are not. Send students on a scavenger hunt to discover more about using capital letters.

Have them look for words around the classroom with capital letters. Write their words on the chalkboard and discuss the reason for each capital letter. Have children continue their hunt at home. Make a chart for children to complete, listing each of the following five categories: Names of People; Titles That Go With Names; Titles of Books, Songs, Magazines, or Movies; Days and Months; Names of Products. Challenge children to find at least one example for each category. For extra credit, they can look for examples that show more ways to use capital letters. Create a class chart that combines students' examples of capital letters with rules for using them.

MATH

Who Loves Ice Cream?

Who in the classroom shares Pattie's passion for ice cream? Take a simple survey to find out. Ask: "Who loves ice cream?" (Count hands.) "Who doesn't?" (Count hands.) Children will surely want to share their favorite flavors, so you'll need to conduct a second survey. For more fun with ice cream, make "sundaes" to explore the relationship between combinations and multiplication.

◆ Give each child a copy of page 42. Have children color each scoop of ice cream to represent a flavor, and the toppings according to the labels. Then have them cut out each sundae ingredient.

◆ Ask children to guess how many different ways they could combine the ingredients to make sundaes. Start with one scoop of ice cream and any two toppings. Ask: "How many combinations of a single scoop and a single topping could you make?" (1 scoop x 2 toppings = 2 combinations)

◆ Add a second scoop to the choices. Ask: "Now how many combinations of a single scoop and a single topping could you make?" (2 scoops x 2 toppings = 4 combinations)

◆ Experiment with more scoops and toppings—for example, making sundaes with two scoops and three toppings.

Who Loves Ice Cream?

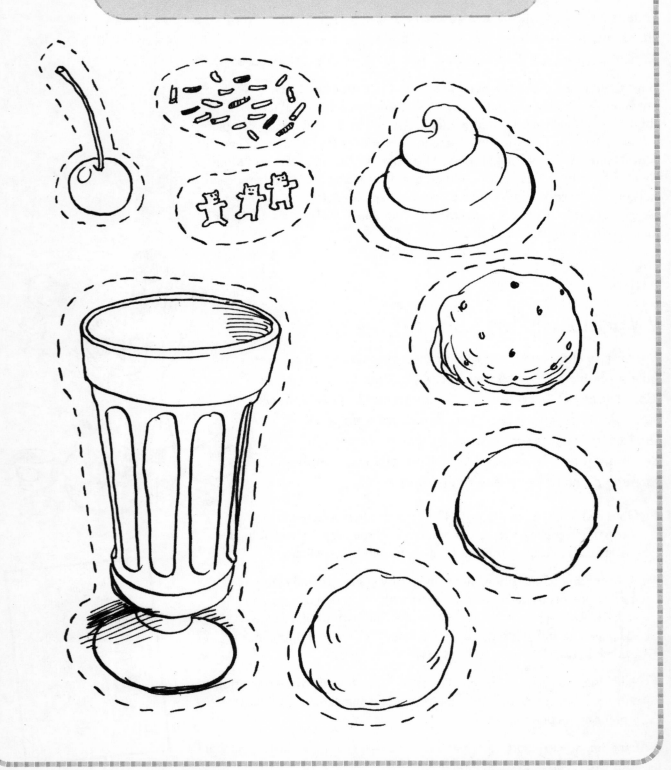

Teaching With the Rib-Tickling Poetry of Douglas Florian   Scholastic Teaching Resources

March In

In like a lion
Out like a lamb,
And when the winds blow
The people all scram.
But March winds will wind down.
And March winds will pass.
And then little lambs
Will graze upon grass.

—*Douglas Florian*

Are students unfamiliar with any words in this poem? The words *scram* and *graze* might be new to some. Let students share what they think these words mean and how other words in the poem can help them figure out the meaning. For example, blowing winds might make people hurry away, or *scram*.

TEACHING connections

- ◆ vocabulary
- ◆ homographs
- ◆ wind

LANGUAGE ARTS

Winds Wind Down

What do students notice about the words *winds* and *wind* in line five of the poem?

Take the *-s* off *winds* and say both words together. One has a short *i* sound and one has a long *i* sound. But they're spelled the same. One is the word for a weather condition; *wind down* means to decrease. Words that are spelled the same but have different meanings and sometimes pronunciations are called homographs. Can students think of more? (for example, *present, can, saw,* and *lean*) Write homographs on slips of paper and place them in a bag. Have pairs of students secretly select a homograph and use it both ways in a sentence. Let students take turns writing their sentences on the chalkboard, leaving blanks for the homographs. Can their classmates guess the missing words?

MATH ◆ SCIENCE

Calendar Connections

Investigate windy weather in the month of March by tracking it on a calendar.

Rate the wind's strength each day: Is it a lion wind or a lamb wind? (You can use a weather report for this, place a wind sock outside the classroom window to observe, or notice the way leaves in trees are blowing.) Make multiple photocopies of the lion and lamb calendar markers (left). Have children glue a lion or lamb picture to the class calendar each day to represent the wind strength. As the weeks progress, let students guess if the wind at the end of the month will be more like a lion or a lamb.

SCIENCE ◆ MOVEMENT

Lions or Lambs?

Play a movement game to help students understand the expression "March comes in like a lion, and goes out like a lamb."

First, reread the poem. Ask: "Is a lion wind strong or gentle? How is a lamb wind different?" Invite students to share their ideas. (*Lions are large, fierce animals, so a "lion" wind is strong; lambs are soft, baby animals, so a "lamb" wind is gentle.*) Then use a large fan to let students act out lion and lamb winds. Have children gather a safe distance from the fan. Turn the fan on high and let children be the lion wind. Lower the speed and let children "graze upon grass" like little lambs.

Sweater Weather

When we have inclement weather
Clearly you should wear a sweather.
Or should I say wear a sweater
When the weater's cold and wetter?
Whether the weather's wetter or better,
It's better to weather the weather with sweaters.

—*Douglas Florian*

The wordplay in this activity will have children repeating the poem again and again for tongue-twisting fun. Some of the wordplay comes from taking liberties with the spelling of a couple of words. Copy the poem on chart paper, being careful to leave the spelling of *sweather* (line 2) and *weater* (line 4) intact. Tell students that the poet intentionally misspelled some words in the poem. Challenge them to spot those words and write them on a slip of paper. Read through children's guesses. Review words students thought were incorrect but are, in fact, correct. Then let them tell how they think *sweather* and *weater* are really spelled. For an interesting discussion, have students guess why they think the poet misspelled these words.

TEACHING Connections

◆ wordplay
◆ synonyms
◆ homonyms

LANGUAGE ARTS

An Inclement Word Wall

What makes the weather in this poem inclement? It's cold and wet!
Learn more weather words with this vocabulary-building activity.

Let students use the context of the poem to guess the meaning of the word
inclement. Then brainstorm other words for inclement weather—for example,
wintry, nippy, brisk, chilly, frosty, stormy, and *icy.* Let children illustrate these
words to make an inclement word wall.

BOOK break

Even dogs wear sweaters sometimes. But when it's a silly sweater covered
with roses, that's another story. In **No Roses for Harry!**, by Gene Zion
(HarperTrophy, 1976), Harry receives such a sweater as a birthday present from
his well-intentioned grandmother, and the plot takes several amusing twists and
turns as he tries to make the gift disappear without hurting anyone's feelings.

LANGUAGE ARTS

Homonym Hunt

Homonyms are confusing to children, who are always trying to learn
tricks for remembering if it's *too, to,* or *two; there, their,* or *they're;*
and in the case of this poem, *whether* or *weather.* Send students
on a homonym hunt to help them recognize the correct use for
words that sound alike but have different spellings and meanings.

◆ Write common homonyms on the chalkboard. Include those from the
poem: *weather/whether, wear/where, to/too/two.* Review the different
meanings/uses.

◆ Give pairs of students a story from the newspaper (or from a magazine).
Challenge children to find as many of the listed homonyms as they can
in their story and highlight each one. Have children give themselves one
point for each homonym they find. You might set a class goal: to have
children find a combined total of 100 homonyms. As a bonus, they can
double the points if they find a homonym that is not listed.

Package

Spring arrived today
Special delivery.
Sent Winter packing
Shaking and shivery.

—*Douglas Florian*

Word Hunt

Explore the sounds in this short spring poem to help students learn more about the devices poets use to get every word just right. Copy the poem on chart paper and read it aloud. Ask students to reread it quietly to themselves, listening for beginning sounds that repeat. They'll find two sets of repeating beginning sounds—the *sp-* in *spring* and *special*, and the *sh-* in *shaking* and *shivery*. (Technically, *spring* begins with the consonant cluster *spr-* and *special* begins with the consonant cluster *sp-*; however, students will hear the letters *sp-* at the beginning of both.) Introduce alliteration, and work together to create a definition based on this example. (*Alliteration is the repetition of beginning consonant sounds in words that are close together.*) Pair up students to extend the word hunt to other poems. What other examples of alliteration can they find? Discuss why this is an effective device for poets to use. (*Poems use relatively few words, so each one must be carefully chosen for meaning, effect, sound, and so on.*)

TEACHING connections

◆ alliteration
◆ seasons
◆ time

LANGUAGE ARTS

Spring Tree

Buds bursting on trees is one sure sign of spring. After reading "Package" and discussing signs of spring, share Douglas Florian's "Tree" (right), which highlights one of the sure signs of spring— leaves "springing" from the branches of trees.

After reading aloud the poem and enjoying the rhythmic structure, ask: "What parts of the tree were named?" (*trunk, branch, stem, leaf*) "Which was not named?" (*the veins inside the leaf that carry fluids or nutrients for the tree*) "What does the poet call this part of the leaf?" (*rivers and oceans of life*)

Introduce *metaphor*, a figure of speech in which two things are compared without using *like* or *as*. In this poem, the metaphor at the end shifts the rhythm of the poem from the simple, repetitive lines to the miraculous—the rivers and oceans of life inside the leaf.

Tree

Out of the earth
Springs a trunk.
Out of the trunk
Springs a branch.
Out of the branch
Springs a stem.
Out of the stem
Springs a leaf.
Inside the leaf
Are rivers
And oceans
Of life.

— Douglas Florian

BOOK break

For a timeless look at a tree in spring and other seasons, share *Sky Tree*, by Thomas Locker (HarperCollins, 1995). Part of the Seeing Science Through Art series, this book follows the wondrous changes in a tree and the sky around it—including the golden spring sun that warms the tree in spring as buds uncurl into leaves.

SOCIAL STUDIES

Seasons Are Special

Spring sent winter packing. What season will send spring packing? Reinforce the concept of seasons—and the passage of time—with a game that celebrates what is special about each.

◆ Write the name of each season on a tagboard shape that represents that season. (For example, cut out a snowflake shape for winter, a flower for spring, a sun for summer, and a pumpkin for fall.)

◆ Tape these season signs on the wall in four different corners of the classroom. Write special characteristics of each season on index cards (one per card). These might include holidays, special events, and symbols.

◆ Give each child a card. Have children decide which season they belong in and move to that sign. Provide multiple calendars, including a class calendar that lists special school events, for reference. When children have all found their places, let them share the special characteristics of their seasons.

SCIENCE

What's Inside?

What would students expect to find inside a spring "package"? Discuss changes that happen as winter comes to a close and spring begins.

What are the familiar signs of spring? What other things do students associate with spring? Let each child make a "package" by tying ribbon to make a bow and gluing it to the top of a sheet of paper. Have children copy the poem on their paper. Then have them fill the package with pictures that represent spring—for example, birds, buds, a baseball, tiny flowers, the sun, baby animals, and eggs. Display students' package pictures for a cheerful spring welcome.

Tip

For an independent follow-up, place the cards at a center for children to sort on their own.

BOOK break

Celebrate the season with *Mud Flat Spring*, by James Stevenson (Greenwillow, 1999), the fifth in the lively Mud Flat series. The characters in this book's nine short stories might be animals, but young readers will relate to their personalities and find their conversations familiar. See how they celebrate spring (or sleep through it, as the case may be), then plan a celebration of your own.

April

April is rain.
April is showers.
April is filling
The world full of flowers.
April is bursting.
April is blooming.
April is when
All the green starts resuming.

—*Douglas Florian*

Word Hunt

Have children hunt for the four words in the poem that end in *-ing*. Then challenge them to decide which of those words has a rule for adding the *-ing* that is different than the rule for the other three words. Take a vote: How many think it is *filling? Bursting? Blooming? Resuming?* Discuss with students reasons for selecting any of those words. Then guide them to recognize that the first three have the ending *-ing* added directly to the base word, without adding or dropping any letters. With *resuming*, the silent *-e* at the end of *resume* is dropped before adding *-ing*. For an independent follow-up, have students complete page 52. Bring students together to discuss the rule that applies to each word.

TEACHING Connections

◆ inflectional endings
◆ vocabulary
◆ data analysis

LANGUAGE ARTS ◆ SCIENCE

Describing Rain

What are some ways to describe rain? Use the poem as a springboard for exploring descriptive language.

Brainstorm ways to say it's raining. How about sprinkling, drizzling, spitting, or coming down in buckets? Then invite children to ask their families if they know of more ways to describe rain. Compile ideas on a class chart. When it rains, let children use the chart to choose the most accurate description for the precipitation.

MATH ◆ SCIENCE

Rainy Day Data

How many children have heard the expression "April showers bring May flowers"? April is often thought of as a rainy month. Find out if it really is with this calendar activity.

◆ Before April begins, pose this question to students: "Will we have more days in April with or without rain?" Write this question at the top of a sheet of chart paper. To show their prediction, have students write their names under the heading "More Days With Rain" or "More Days Without Rain."

◆ During your morning calendar routine, ask children if it rained the previous day. If it did, have them color a raindrop on that calendar date.

◆ At the end of the month, ask students to count the raindrops. Have them find out how that number compares with the total number of days in the month. (30) Were more or fewer than half the days in April rainy?

BOOK break

For more rainy-day poetry, share Jack Prelutsky's **Rainy, Rainy, Saturday** (Greenwillow, 1980). For another poetic look at rain, share **Rain Drop Splash**, by Alvin Tresselt (Mulberry, 1990), a Caldecott honor book that follows rain from puddles to streams, rivers, and oceans.

Tip

Resuming may be a new word for students, so be sure to discuss its meaning after sharing the poem. Let students suggest words with a similar meaning, such as *beginning again* (which gives you a chance to discuss another rule for adding -ing!)

Adding -ing!

Name _____   Date _____

Look at each picture. Fill in the missing letters to tell what is going on in each picture. Write the base word underneath. Draw a new picture in the last box to show you doing something. Write the -ing word that tells what you're doing. Write the root word underneath.

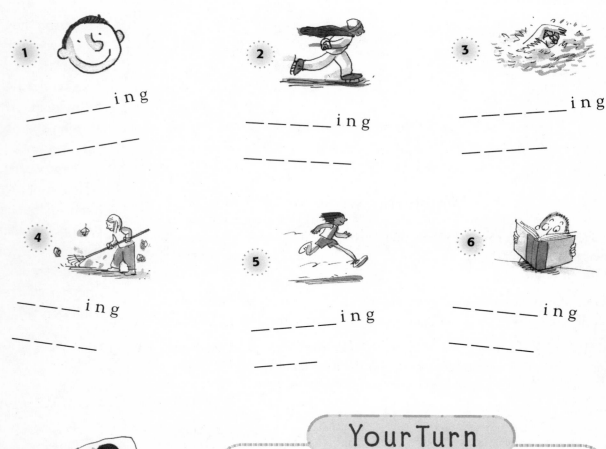

1 _ _ _ _ i n g
   _ _ _ _

2 _ _ _ _ _ i n g
   _ _ _ _

3 _ _ _ _ _ _ i n g
   _ _ _ _

4 _ _ _ _ i n g
   _ _ _ _

5 _ _ _ _ _ i n g
   _ _ _

6 _ _ _ _ _ i n g
   _ _ _ _

Your Turn

7  _ _ _ _ _ i n g
   _ _ _ _ _

Draw a new picture. Write the -ing word and the root word.

┌─────────────┐   _____
│   │   -ing word
│   │
│   │   _____
└─────────────┘   root word

Rain

One drop
    Two drops
Three drops
    Four.
Soon the skies will
Start to pour.
    Five drops
Six drops.
    Seven drops.
Eight.
    Watch the world
Precipitate.

—*Douglas Florian*

Word Hunt

Copy the poem on chart paper and read it aloud. Then send students on a word hunt: Can they find four words in the poem that sound like other words but are spelled differently and have different meanings? (*one, four, pour, eight*) Homonyms often present spelling challenges to students: Is it *one* or *won? Four* or *fore? Pour* or *poor? Eight* or *ate?* Play a game that reinforces meaning and spelling: Have children write each pair of homonyms on an index card (one word per side). Use one of the words in a sentence. Have children hold up the correct card, with the corresponding word facing out. Repeat the procedure to review each word in context. Let children take over if they're ready—using the words in context and having classmates hold up the correct spelling.

TEACHING Connections

- spelling
- water cycle
- clouds

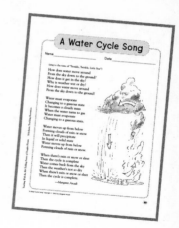

Tip

While the concept of water changing form may be difficult for children to grasp, this song lays the foundation for understanding that water is still water, in all of its forms.

MUSIC ◆ SCIENCE

A Water Cycle Song

Rain is part of the water cycle. Learn more with a piggyback song.

Give each child a copy of page 55. Review challenging vocabulary first—for example, *evaporate*, *gaseous*, and *precipitate* (which children may recognize from the poem)—then sing the song together.

SCIENCE

Cleanup Clouds

Investigate clouds to learn that some bring rain—and some don't.

As a class, record weather conditions and what the clouds look like over a period of time. Stratus (low and layered) and cumulonimbus clouds (dark thunderclouds) bring rain. Cirrus (wispy) and cumulous clouds (fluffy, white) are seen in sunny skies. Squirt shaving cream on each child's desk. Let children form the shaving cream into cirrus and cumulous clouds first. Then lightly tint the shaving cream with black tempera paint. Make rain clouds!

MATH ◆ SCIENCE

Rain Reign

Share another poem by Douglas Florian about rain (right). If it *were* raining "cats and dogs," how much rain do students think would fall in one hour? Find out!

Rain Reign

It started raining cats and dogs
Then hares and bears and bats and hogs
By four it poured down dinosaurs—
Some days it pays to stay indoors.

—*Douglas Florian*

On a tall, clear jar, mark inches and fractions of inches in permanent marker. In a wide-mouth jar, such as a peanut butter jar, place a large funnel. When it rains, set the wide-mouth jar outside in an open area for 30 minutes. Remove the funnel and pour the rain into the tall jar. How much did it rain in 30 minutes? What is the rate of rainfall for one hour?

A Water Cycle Song

Name_____   Date_____

(sing to the tune of "Twinkle, Twinkle, Little Star")

How does water move around
From the sky down to the ground?
How does it get in the sky?
Why is weather wet or dry?
How does water move around
From the sky down to the ground?

Water must evaporate
Changing to a gaseous state
It becomes a cloudy mass
When the water turns to gas
Water must evaporate
Changing to a gaseous state.

Water moves up from below
Forming clouds of rain or snow
Then it will precipitate
In liquid or solid state
Water moves up from below
Forming clouds of rain or snow.

When there's rain or snow or sleet
Then the cycle is complete
Water comes back from the sky
Then the weather's not so dry
When there's rain or snow or sleet
Then the cycle is complete.

—Margaret Arcadi

I'm in the Mood for Mud

I'm in the mood for mud—
I'm mad for sloggy, boggy crud.
I wish to wallow in a mire,
To slip and slosh my heart's desire.
To slide and slop inside the slush,
To run amok amid the mush.
And when I'm done I'll run upstairs,
Where in the tub I'll wash my hairs,
And back and legs and arms and chin,
Then run back in the mud again.

—*Douglas Florian*

Word Hunt

Because poetry is composed of relatively few words (compared to a story), every word counts even more than usual. Invite children to identify the words in the poem that help readers paint a picture of playing in mud (*slip, slosh, slide, slop,* and so on). Let students use a thesaurus to find other words that the poet might have used to bring mud to life. Choose a new topic related to this time of year—for example, rain. Invite children to brainstorm words that help paint a picture of rain, such as *drip, drizzle,* and *drench.* Find more words with a thesaurus!

TEACHING Connections

- ◆ word choice
- ◆ apostrophes
- ◆ soil

LANGUAGE ARTS

It's an Apostrophe!

Young children enjoy using apostrophes in their early writing. Use the poem as an introduction to a more formal lesson on these curly characters.

◆ Read the poem aloud. Let students take turns using a pointer to find words with apostrophes, including *I'm* (three times), *I'll* (two times), and *heart's*.

◆ Review contractions (two words put together so they make a shortened form). Review possessives (to indicate ownership).

◆ Ask volunteers to find contractions in the poem and to write the two words that form each contraction. Model the process of forming a contraction by putting the apostrophe where the letter is left out. Guide children to notice that sometimes more than one letter is left out (as in *I'll*).

◆ Write "heart's desire" on the chalkboard. Discuss with children whether the apostrophe is used to make a contraction or to show possession.

◆ Let students work with partners to find examples of contractions and possessives in reading materials. (You might ask each pair to find five of each.) Have students keep a list of words they find. Bring students together to share their findings. Pay special attention to contractions that are unusual, such as *I'd* (I would), *won't* (will not), and *should've* (should have).

SCIENCE

Recipe for Mud

What makes the best mud? Find out with a simple but captivating science experiment.

◆ Have students pair up. Give each pair a shallow container, $\frac{1}{4}$ cup dry soil (you can have this premeasured in resealable sandwich bags or let students measure it), an eye dropper, a container of water, a craft stick, and a record sheet for each child.

◆ Ask students to predict how much water they'll need to add to make perfect mud. Have them record their predictions.

◆ Have students add water one drop at a time and stir with the craft stick. Ask students to use words and/or pictures to record observations as the soil changes to mud.

Tip

Uncooked elbow noodles make an apostrophe statement! As children use sentences with apostrophes in their own writing, have them copy them on sentence strips and glue the noodles in place to form contractions or show possession. Display the sentence strips on a bulletin board with a border full of elbow-noodle apostrophes.

Recipe for Mud

Name _____ Date _____

1 Prediction $\frac{1}{4}$ cup soil + [   ] drops of water = perfect mud

2 Data Keep a tally of the drops of water you add to the soil. How does the soil change with each addition of water? Record your observations at different stages.

Drops of Water	Observations

3 Results $\frac{1}{4}$ cup soil + [   ] drops of water = perfect mud

Teaching With the Rib-Tickling Poetry of Douglas Florian   Scholastic Teaching Resources

May

In May you may plant.
In May you may play.
In May you may work hard
At nothing all day.

—*Douglas Florian*

Word Hunt

How many times can children find the word *may* in this four-line poem? Six times— three of those are capitalized and three are not. Ask children why this word appears both ways. (*In the first use in each sentence, the word* May *refers to the month and so is capitalized. In the second use in each sentence, the word* may *is used to indicate possibility and so does not require capitalization.*)

TEACHING Connections

- capitalization
- commonly misused words
- calendars

LANGUAGE ARTS

Can I? May I?

"Can I go to the bathroom?" When children ask if they can do something, they are often guided to rephrase their question using *may* instead. Use the poem as a springboard for learning the difference.

Can and *may* are commonly misused words—one refers to having the ability to do something, the other is used to ask permission. Start a class word wall of commonly misused words. Use read-alouds and students' own writing as a source of these words. A sampling of words you might include are *desert* and *dessert*, *its* and *it's*, *lay* and *lie*, *loose* and *lose*, *principal* and *principle*, *right* and *write*, *passed* and *past*, and *than* and *then*. Have students list the word at the top of the page, use it correctly in a sentence, and give the meaning.

SOCIAL STUDIES ◆ LANGUAGE ARTS

What Can You Say About May?

What made the news in the month of May? Send students on a scavenger hunt to find out.

◆ Ask children to find out something that happened in the month of May that they didn't know before—and that they think will be news to their classmates, too. For example, on May 5, 1904, Cy Young pitched the first perfect baseball game—nobody on the opposite team made it to first base!

◆ Give each child two sticky notes (leave them stuck together). Have children lift the first sticky note and write their fun fact on the sticky note underneath.

◆ Place the notes one per square on the class calendar. Peel off the top sticky note each day to reveal something new about the month of May!

BOOK break

May (*It Happens in the Month of*), by Ellen B. Jackson (Charlesbridge, 2002), is full of fun facts about the month of May—including weather information, animal behavior, holidays, birthdays of famous people, and historical events.

The Inchworm

I inch, I arch, I march along. I'm just a pinch, a mere inch long. I stroll and stick on sticks in thickets, and never pick up speeding tickets.

—Douglas Florian

Word Hunt

Arch, march . . . pinch, inch . . . stick, pick . . . thickets, tickets…. "The Inchworm" is full of pairs of words that have letter clusters in common. Invite children to hunt for words like this. Let them share their words with the class and explain what they noticed about the words. For example, children might notice that *pinch* is spelled the same as *inch* with a *p* added at the beginning. They might see that if you take the *h* out of *thickets*, it spells *tickets*. Use children's findings as beginnings of mini-lessons to reinforce spelling patterns, phonics skills, and more.

TEACHING Connections

- ◆ measurement
- ◆ vocabulary (synonyms)
- ◆ insects

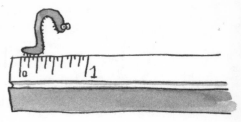

MATH ◆ LANGUAGE ARTS

Measuring Worm

If students were going to rename
the inchworm, what name would they
give it? Write their suggestions on
chart paper. Did anyone suggest calling an inchworm a *measuring
worm*? If not, add it to the list. Students might be surprised
to learn that *measuring worm* is another name for inchworm!
Check the definition in the dictionary. Then let children explore
measurement with their own inchworms.

◆ Invite children to look around the classroom and name things they think
are about the same size as an inchworm. List suggestions on the chalkboard.

◆ Give each child a copy of page 63. Have children color and cut out the
inchworm and use it to measure the items on the list. Have them record
their findings on the record sheet.

◆ To go further, invite children to take their inchworm home and measure
more things. Ask them to record both the items and their measurements.
Let children share their findings with the class.

MUSIC ◆ SCIENCE

What's an Insect? What's Not?

An inchworm, not surprisingly, is a kind of caterpillar. Let students
discover more about this moth larvae with this activity:

Sing a song about insects. (See right.)
Then invite students to decide, after
looking at a picture, whether or not an
inchworm is an insect. (An inchworm
is a moth caterpillar. Unlike other
moth larvae, this insect has legs at the
front and rear but not in the middle.)
Provide pictures of other insects and
creepy crawlies, such as spiders (which
are not insects, but arachnids). Have
students use what they know to classify
them as insects or not insects.

I'm a Little Insect

(sing to the tune of
"I'm a Little Teapot")

I'm a little insect with six legs
I crawl or fly and I lay eggs
I might be small or long or fat
But I don't belong with spiders
Remember that!

— *Margaret Arcadi*

Tip

Try the activity
with items children
think are smaller
than an inch.
Guide children
in using the
fractional
segments of
an inch on a
ruler to check
measurements.

Measuring Worm

Name _____ Date _____

Item	Longer Than 1 inch	Shorter Than 1 inch	The Same as 1 inch

1 inch

Flower Power

Maury loves a morning glory.
Maisy favors daisies.
Joey grows geraniums.
For tulips Tal is crazy.

Lyle likes his violets.
Lila likes a lily.
Willy's wild for wallflowers.
Bluebells make Bill silly.

Petra plants petunias.
Flax with Max agrees.
But poor Louise
Is hard to please:
For flowers make her sneeze.

—*Douglas Florian*

Word Hunt

If flowers didn't make Louise sneeze, what would her favorite flower be? Before students decide, repeat the following names and flowers: Maury/morning glory; Tal/tulips; Lila/lily; Willy/wallflower; and Petra/petunias. What do these pairs of words have in common? (*The name and the flower in each pair start with the same letter.*) If flowers didn't make Louise sneeze, what flower would make a good match for her? Let students suggest names for flowers that start with the letter *l*, such as lupine, lady's slipper, or lilac.

TEACHING connections

◆ phonics (initial sounds)
◆ flowers
◆ attributes

64

LANGUAGE ARTS ◆ SCIENCE

A Flower for Me

Once students find a flower for Louise, they'll be eager to pair their own names with flowers that start with the same sound.

Provide resources for looking up flower names. (See Tip, right.) Once students have selected a flower, ask them to draw a picture of it, being careful to pay attention to such attributes as color, shape and number of petals, leaves, stems, and size. Have them use the poem as a model for writing a sentence to go with the picture—for example, "Ben goes bananas for begonias." Have children copy their alliterative lines on sentence strips, then put them together to create a class poem. Use students' flower pictures for the sorting activity that follows.

SCIENCE ◆ MATH

Flower Sort

Bring children together in a seated circle for a sorting activity that explores attributes of flowers.

Use yarn to create a Venn diagram in the center of the circle. Ask students to share attributes of their flowers (from the above activity)—for example, six petals; red, fuzzy leaves; yellow center. Write the various attributes on index cards and choose two to label the Venn diagram. Let children take turns considering the groupings and deciding where their flower belongs: in the overlapping section of the circles (their flower has both characteristics), in one circle or the other (their flower shares one of the characteristics), or on the outside of both circles (their flower has neither characteristic). Change the Venn diagram labels and repeat the activity to discover other ways students' flowers are alike and different.

Tip

Students will find lots of flowers to consider (more than 150) in **National Audubon Society First Field Guides: Flowers** (Scholastic, 1998). The National Gardening Association children's Web site **(www.kidsgardening. com)** has dozens of stories and activities about flowers, as well as answers to questions.

BOOK break

For another playful look at names and flowers, share **Alison's Zinnia**, by Anita Lobel (Greenwillow, 1990). In this alphabet book, Alison acquires an amaryllis for Beryl, who buys a begonia for Crystal, and so on. As you read the circular story, have students try to figure out how the children's names and flowers are connected. The end takes readers right back to the beginning, with Zena zeroing in on a zinnia for Alison.

School's Out

No more teachers.
No more books.
But sometimes when nobody looks
I sneak inside the library
To peek at books on history,
Or science fiction,
Summer reading.
Don't tell the other kids
I'm cheating.

—*Douglas Florian*

TEACHING connections

- spelling patterns
- genres
- summer reading

Word Hunt

Summer . . . . What's the first thing that comes to students' minds when they hear that word? They might think of double letters after this activity. Ask children what's special about the word *summer*. Guide them to recognize the double *m*. Ask students to find other words in the poem with double letters. (*school's, books, looks, peek, tell*) Ask children which double-letter words rhyme. (*books, looks*) Find and say each word with a double *o*. (*school's, books, looks*) Do they all have the same vowel sound? (*No,* books *and* looks *sound the same, but* school *has a different sound.*)

LANGUAGE ARTS

What Are We Reading?

How often do students choose a history book from the library shelves? Science fiction? After a trip to the library, make a graph to explore the various genres students select. Use the data to encourage children to sample books from a variety of genres.

◆ Write various genres on index cards, one per card. (Fiction, Science Fiction, Fantasy, Poetry, Nonfiction)

◆ Tape the index cards across the bottom of the chalkboard. Have children take turns writing the titles of books they borrowed from the library above the corresponding genre.

◆ Follow up by discussing the data and sharing with students some books they might like that are from less widely read genres.

MATH ◆ LANGUAGE ARTS

Summer Reading Calendar Countdown

When is school out for your students? Have them estimate the number of days, then count on a school calendar to find out. Keep students focused on learning with a lift-the-flap calendar that lets children count down to those vacation days and inspires summer reading at the same time.

◆ Cover a bulletin board with craft paper. Mark off a calendar grid and fill in the dates for the last month of school.

◆ In each school day square, write the first sentence of a story you think your students might like to read. Include the title and author. Cover each square with a construction paper flap (or sticky note), and write the date on it.

◆ Each day, invite a child to lift the corresponding flap and read the sentence aloud, along with the title and author. Have children record the title and author on a "School's Out" reading list. By the end of the year, they'll have a fun summer reading list!

Good Sport

I like to run
Out in the sun.
It makes me squint
Each time I sprint.
And while I walk
I sometimes talk.
I jump and jog
Over a log.
For a change of pace
I may just race.
And then I rest.
(That feels the best.)

—*Douglas Florian*

Wiggle, Squirm, Skip

Run, *sun, squint, sprint* . . . This poem is packed with verbs. Invite children to identify all the words in the poem that describe an action. (*run, sun, squint, sprint, walk, talk, jump, jog, race, rest*) Notice the rhyming pairs of verbs, then invite students to think of more verbs that rhyme. A good way to begin is to brainstorm words for the ways children move—for example, they *wiggle, squirm, dance, leap, slide, skip, twist,* and *stomp.* Write these on the chalkboard. Challenge children to find rhyming partners for some of the words—for example, *slide* and *collide; skip* and *flip.*

TEACHING Connections

- verbs
- vocabulary
- safety

MOVEMENT ◆ LANGUAGE ARTS

Walk, Wiggle, Waltz!

Reinforce understanding of parts of speech with an activity that builds vocabulary for action words—and lets children get from one place to another with some very interesting movements!

On foot-shaped cards, write words for the ways students could move. Place them in a bag or other container. When it's time to line up for lunch or another activity outside the classroom, invite a student to select a card at random from the container. Have this student demonstrate the verb and then lead the class to its destination, with everyone moving as indicated. Students will eagerly incorporate this descriptive vocabulary into their own writing to bring their writing to life.

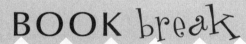

BOOK break

Add to your exploration of action words with **To Root, to Toot, to Parachute: What Is a Verb?** by Brian Cleary (Carolrhoda, 2001). Students will enjoy adding on to the alliterative pairs of verbs in this fast-paced book.

HEALTH AND SAFETY ◆ LANGUAGE ARTS

Playground Safety Game

With all that running, sprinting, jumping, and jogging, there are bound to be some bumps and bruises. Children typically spend more time outside in the summer, increasing their risk for injuries during outdoor activities. Share an excerpt from "The Swing." Then play a game of follow the leader to reinforce safety rules.

◆ Invite children to picture themselves on a swing as you read aloud a favorite peom (right). Ask children how high they went in their imaginary swing. Then discuss swingset safety rules—for example, "Only go as high as you feel comfortable," and "Don't walk in front of someone on a swing."

◆ Go outside for a game of follow the leader. Let children take turns leading the group to a piece of playground equipment, and then sharing and demonstrating rules for playing on it. Repeat the activity until all have been explored.

The Swing

How do you like to go up in a swing
Up in the air so blue?
Oh, I do think it the pleasantest thing
Ever a child can do!

—*Robert Louis Stevenson*

Sandy

Sand on the beach.
Sand on my legs.
Sand on my sandwich
And sand on the eggs.
Sand in my sandals.
Sand in my feet.
Sand in our car
As we roll down the street.
Sand on the sidewalk.
Sand through the door.
Sand on the walls
And sand on the floor.
Sand on the stairs.
Sand in my bed.
Sand from the Sandman
As dreams fill my head.

—*Douglas Florian*

TEACHING connections

◆ spelling patterns

◆ problem solving

◆ attributes

Sand is everywhere in this poem—on the beach, legs, eggs, feet, and so on. How many times does the word *sand* appear? Let students count (14). Then ask them how many words contain the smaller word *sand* in them. (3) Let students use pointers to highlight these words. Then challenge children to find other words within words in this poem. There's *an* and *and* in *sand*; *be* and *each* in *beach*; *tree* in *street*; *side*, *dew*, and *walk* in *sidewalk*; and more! Guide children to understand that noticing words within words can help them read and write new words.

LANGUAGE ARTS

Sand Math

There's something about sand that is irresistible to children. Whether they're digging in it, sifting it through their fingers, or making mud cakes with it, children are always eager to get their hands on sand. Here's a fun, sandy setup that will have children digging in sand to practice addition and subtraction skills.

◆ Fill a large tub or water table with play sand. Fill a bucket with small shells.

◆ Together, count the shells in the bucket. Ask children to close their eyes while you bury some of the shells. When they open their eyes, show them the shells in the bucket. Ask: "How many shells did I bury in the sand?"

◆ Let children share their answers and reasoning. Then let them take turns digging for shells in the sand to check their answers.

◆ Discuss with students how they can use both addition and subtraction to find out how many shells are in the sand.

◆ Let children repeat the activity with partners, taking turns burying some shells and having their partners tell how many shells they'll find in the sand.

ART ◆ SOCIAL STUDIES

Sand Art

In what other places can students find sand? It's not just in the sandbox and in children's shoes.

Sand is used to make bricks and pots. Mix up some sand clay to try making these and other things in the classroom: Combine equal parts play sand, cornstarch, and hot water (teacher only). Stir until cool. Invite children to experiment with the sand clay—for example, cutting it into mini-bricks to build structures or shaping it into small pots. To harden clay creations, bake at 300° F for one hour.

Tip

Sand Art was adapted from **Hands-On Math Around the Year**, by Jacqueline Clarke (Scholastic, 2000), which includes more activities on sand.

The Summer Trees

The winter trees are sparse and spare.
You barely see a bird up there.
But after the spring equinox
There's flocks
   and flocks
      and flocks
         and flocks.

—*Douglas Florian*

Word Hunt

This short poem is packed with consonant clusters (two or three consonants that appear consecutively in a word; each consonant retains its sound when blended). Say the words *spot*, *spoon*, *speak*, and *spin*. Ask students to find two words in the poem that start with the same sound. Write *sparse* and *spare* on the chalkboard and underline the letters *sp*. Let children notice that in each case, the letter combination *sp-* always stands for the same blended sound. Repeat the activity with the words *spring* (consonant cluster *spr-*), *tree* (consonant cluster *tr-*), and *flock* (consonant cluster *fl-*). Start consonant cluster word walls, choosing a concrete example and including a picture for the lead word to help students remember the sound-spelling relationships.

TEACHING connections

- phonics (consonant blends/clusters)
- collective nouns
- operations

LANGUAGE ARTS ◆ SCIENCE

Flock, Pack, Pride

What's a group of birds called? After reading the poem, students might correctly guess *flock*. What other names for groups of animals do they know?

Write the following words for groups of animals on one side of the chalkboard and, in random order, the corresponding animals on the other. Let students guess which animal goes with each name:

gaggle (geese)	school (fish)	pride (lions)
pod (whales)	shiver (sharks)	crash (rhinoceri)
herd (cows or horses)	mob (kangaroos)	pack (wolves)

MATH

Flocks in a Tree Math Mat

Let children investigate sets of birds to strengthen addition and multiplication skills.

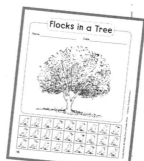

Give each child a copy of page 74. Ask children to color and cut out the birds and tree. Have them glue the tree to a sheet of construction paper. Write a number sentence on the chalkboard—for example, 6 x 3. Invite children to arrange the birds on the tree in "flocks" to represent this number sentence. (In this case, they would place three groups of six birds each in the tree.) Have students share answers to the number sentence and count their birds to check. To go further, have children make new arrangements with their birds and write number sentences to go with them.

Tip

Children can also write word problems about their birds—for example, "Two flocks of five birds each were sitting in the tree. Two birds in each flock flew away from the tree. How many were left in the tree?"— and then trade seats and use the birds to show their solutions.

BOOK break

To investigate more names for various groups of animals, share **A Gaggle of Geese: The Collective Names of the Animal Kingdom**, by Philippa-Alys Browne (Atheneum, 1996). For a comical look at animal groups, share **Herd of Cows! Flock of Sheep!**, by Rick Walton (Gibbs Smith, 2002). In this barnyard tale, Farmer Bob brings in the crops before a big rainstorm and then turns in for a good night's sleep. Find out what happens when the river rises!

Flocks in a Tree

Name_____ Date_____

Teaching With the Rib-Tickling Poetry of Douglas Florian   Scholastic Teaching Resources

Take a Bike

Be careful when you ride your bike
Of people going for a hike.
Steer clear of all geraniums
And pigs and Pomeranians.
Watch out for other bicycles,
Or toddlers on their tricycles,
And snails that slowly cross the street
But most of all of dragons' feet.

—*Douglas Florian*

Word Hunt

Can children spot part of a word that means "two?" How about part of a word that means "three"? Invite them to share the clues they used to figure out what the prefixes *bi-* and *tri-* mean. Then use a dictionary to brainstorm other words that share these prefixes—for example, *binocular, bifocals, binar, biannual, bicuspid, triangle, triple, triathlete, tripod,* and *trivet.* Guide students to be aware of letter clusters that look like prefixes but are not. For example, in *billion* and *trick,* the clusters *bi* and *tri* are not prefixes. Introduce other prefixes that students will encounter in their reading. *Un-, re-, in-, im-, ir-,* and *ill-* are among the most common.

TEACHING connections

- prefixes
- health and safety
- problem solving

Tip

The National Safe Kids Campaign (www.safekids.org) states that wearing a helmet can reduce the risk of head injuries by as much as 88 percent. Correct fit and positioning is essential. Consider inviting a child safety expert (check with your local police department) to visit your class for a helmet check. Invite families to attend, too.

SAFETY ◆ MATH

Helmet Parade

Promote the importance of wearing helmets while bike riding or doing other activities—such as playing baseball (the batter's helmet), skateboarding, in-line skating, skiing, hockey, football, and snowboarding—by having a Helmet Day.

◆ Invite students to bring a helmet to school. Display the helmets and discuss the different activities they represent.

◆ Use the helmets to create floor graphs. Graph them by sports. Then try graphing by size, color, and place manufactured.

◆ Let children draw a picture of themselves wearing a favorite helmet as they participate in the corresponding activity. Create a display that includes helmet safety tips—for example, "Ask an adult to make sure the helmet fits correctly."

MATH

How Many Bikes?

Here's a fun, open-ended math problem that lets students explore combinations of two and three:

Give students a copy of page 77. Have them cut out the wheels and children. Explain that the nine children are riding bikes—some are riding two-wheelers, some are riding three-wheelers or tricycles. Invite students to arrange the wheels to represent the bikes the children are riding. Using all of the wheels and children, how many are riding two-wheelers? Three-wheelers? Ask students to set aside the pictures of children. Now have them investigate how many different combinations of two-wheelers and three-wheelers they can make with the 22 wheels, without having any wheels left over. Let students share possible solutions.

BOOK break

Safety on Your Bicycle, by Lucia Raatma (Bridgestone Books, 2000), uses photographs and simple text to teach young readers about proper equipment, safety checks, and rules for riding.

How Many Bikes?

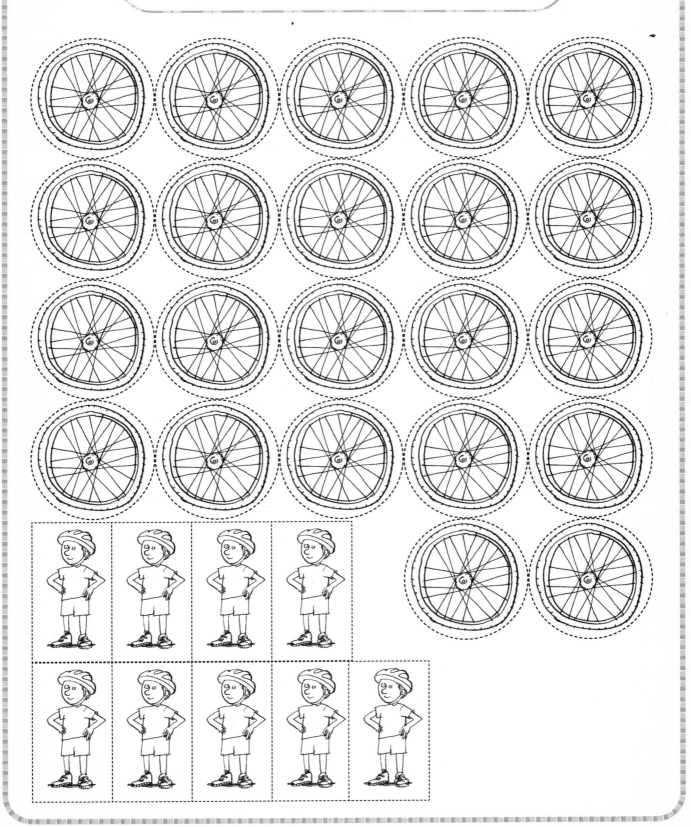

Teaching With the Rib-Tickling Poetry of Douglas Florian   Scholastic Teaching Resources

Eight More Rib-Tickling Poems by

Douglas Florian

Pages 79–80 give students eight more original poems by Douglas Florian. Give each student a copy of these pages. Ask students to cut out the mini-book pages and stack them in order. Have them add a front and back cover, and then staple to bind. In addition to using the suggestions on page 6 (Teaching Activities for Any Time), try these suggestions for teaching with the poems in the mini-book:

Wet Red Leaf: *Meander* will be a new word for many students. Act it out by moving aimlessly about. Ask students to tell what they think the word means. Then let them act out other ways to move while classmates guess the word.

Staying Warm: Let children have fun illustrating this poem and sharing their pictures. Invite children to share ways they bundle up for cold weather. Go further to learn about ways animals—such as bears, penguins, and the meadow mouse—adapt to winter.

Painting the White House: How many dozen gallons of paint does it take to paint the White House? Let students team up to calculate the answer, then share their reasoning with the class.

Groundhog Day: Share *The Story of Punxsutawney Phil, the Fearless Forecaster*, by Julia Spencer Moutran (Crown, 1988). Use the groundhog's forecast as a springboard to learning more about weatherlore with *A January Fog Will Freeze a Hog*, by Hubert Davis, ed. (1977).

Get Pet: Pets are a favorite subject with students. Brainstorm kinds of pets and the care they need. Use charts to compare characteristics of each animal, such as fur/no fur, number of legs, tail/no tail, and so on.

Seedy: Have fun exploring the differences between flowers, fruits, and weeds. If possible, share seeds of each. Look at pictures of the plants and discuss how they are alike and different. Let students write a definition for each: What is a flower? (*rose*) A fruit? (*tomato*) A weed?

Julying: This poem is perfect for making math connections with the number of days in each month. Let children sort them: How many have 30 days? 31? A different number? Teach children the rhyme for learning the number of days in each month. (30 days hath September, April, June, and November. February has 28 alone. All the rest have 31.)

Lemonade! List on chart paper the ingredients in the poem for homemade lemonade: lemon juice, purple ink, ladybugs, salt, pepper, ice. Then work with students to write step-by-step directions for this unusual recipe. Invite students to copy the poem on paper and draw pictures to illustrate each step.

Wet Red Leaf

I saw a wet red leaf meander,
then realized:
A salamander!

—Douglas Florian

1

Staying Warm

It's 15 degrees; there's a nip in the air.
So I opened my drawer, put on long underwear.
I threw on three shirts
And two sweaters, too,
My itchy wool vest
And overcoat (blue),
A super long scarf
(It hangs down to the floor).
Now won't someone help me
To get through the door?

—Douglas Florian

2

Painting the White House

Painting the White House
Five hundred and seventy gallons
Of paint to paint today.
Five hundred and seventy gallons
And—oops, they gave me gray!

—Douglas Florian

3

Groundhog Day

A groundhog first came out today
Came out to see his shadow
Saw all the people looking down
And ran off to the meadow.

—Douglas Florian

4

Get Pet

I'm gentle with my gerbil.
Devoted to my dog.
I check up on my chicken.
I love to hug my hog.
I softly grab my rabbit.
I'm kindly with my cat.
But when I sleep
I always keep
My distance from my bat.

—Douglas Florian

5

Seedy

Rose planted the roses,
Maizy daisy seeds.
Tom planted tomatoes.
Who put in the weeds?

—Douglas Florian

6

Julying

The earth is hot.
The air is thick.
While flies I swat
My clothes all stick.
Thirty one days hath July—
I couldn't skip a few—could I?

—Douglas Florian

7

Lemonade!

Lemonade!
Don't be afraid
It's all homemade!
I mixed it in the kitchen sink
With lemon juice and purple ink
And ladybugs to make it sweet
Then stirred it up with my bare feet.
Threw salt and pepper in for spice.
To keep it cold I added ice.
On sale for just 5 cents a glass.
I hear it helps your head grow grass.

—Douglas Florian

8